INSPIRATIONAL LIVES

KELLY HOLMES

OLYMPIC HEROINE

Simon Hart

WAYLAND

First published in 2011 by Wayland

Copyright © Wayland 2011

Wayland
338 Euston Road
London NW1 3BH

Wayland Australia
Level 17/207 Kent Street
Sydney, NSW 2000

Editor: Nicola Edwards
Designer: Paul Cherrill

Acknowledgements:

British Library cataloguing in
Publication Data
Hart, Simon.
Kelly Holmes : Olympic heroine. --
(Inspirational lives)
   1. Holmes, Kelly--Juvenile literature.
   2. Women track and field
   athletes--Great Britain--Biography--
   Juvenile literature.
   3. Track and field athletes--Great Britain--
   Biography--Juvenile literature.
   I. Title II. Series
   796.4'2'092-dc22

ISBN: 978 0 7502 6480 8

Printed in China

Wayland is a division of Hachette
Children's Books, an Hachette UK
company.

www.hachette.co.uk

Picture acknowledgements: The author
and publisher would like to thank the
following for allowing their pictures
to be reproduced in this publication:
Cover: Scott Barbour/Getty Images;
p4 Michael Steele/Getty Images; p5
Kirsty Wigglesworth/PA Archive/Press
Association Images; p6 John Stillwell/
PA Archive/Press Association Images; p7
Ian West/PA Archive/Press Association
Images; Gareth Fuller/PA Archive/Press
Association Images; p9 Chris Smith/Getty
Images; p10 Getty Images for Norwich
Union; p11 Neil Munns/PA Archive/Press
Association Images; p12 Phil Cole /
Getty Images; p13 Tony Duffy/ALLSPORT
(Getty Images); p14 Mike Powell / Getty
Images; p15 GEORGES GOBET/AFP/Getty
Images; p16 Mike Egerton/EMPICS Sport;
p17 Nick Wilson /Allsport (Getty Images;
p18 Michael Steele/Getty Images; p19
Popperfoto/Getty Images; p20 Mike
Hewitt/Getty Images; p21 Jamie Squire/
Getty Images; p22 PA Photos/PA Archive/
Press Association Images; p23 Kirsty
Wigglesworth/ROTA/Getty Images; p24
Getty Images for Norwich Union; p25 Getty
Images/Getty Images for Norwich Union;
p26 Getty Images for Laureus; p27 Gareth
Cattermole/Getty Images for Laureus; p28
Julian Finney/Getty Images; p29 Getty
Images for Laureus

Contents

Golden girl

In August 2004, in the Greek capital of Athens, Kelly Holmes made sporting history. She became the first British woman to win two gold medals at an Olympic Games when she triumphed on the running track in the 800 and 1500 metres. After a career blighted by injury and illness, her double victory was highly emotional. She admitted she did not know whether to laugh or cry.

WOW!

After Kelly won the 800 metres at the Athens Olympics she went to sleep with the gold medal on her pillow.

Kelly celebrates as she wins the 1500 metres final and her second gold medal at the Athens Olympics in 2004.

Kelly had originally planned to compete in just the 1500 metres in Athens but, at the last minute, she decided to enter both races. It was a big risk for the 34-year-old because of the strain it would put on her body, but she knew she was in the best form of her life. For once, she had arrived at an Olympic Games without any injury problems and she was determined to make the most it.

Her first race was the 800 metres – two laps of the track. This was the bigger challenge of the two events but Kelly ran a perfect race, remaining at the back of the field before surging to the front on the final bend to win the gold medal.

Five days later, Kelly returned to the stadium for the final of the 1500 metres. Again running from the rear of the field, she took the lead in the final **straight** to claim her second Olympic title.

Kelly's achievement earned her another title the following year when she became 'Dame Kelly Holmes' at a ceremony at Buckingham Palace.

Following her Olympic triumph, Kelly chats to the Queen at a reception for Olympic and Paralympic athletes held at Buckingham Palace.

HONOURS BOARD

Women's 800m, 2004 Olympics
1, Kelly Holmes (GB) 1min 56.38sec
2, Hasna Benhassi (Morocco) 1min 56.43sec
3, Jolanda Ceplak (Slovenia) 1min 56.43sec

Women's 1500m, 2004 Olympics
1, Kelly Holmes (GB) 3min 57.90sec (British record)
2, Tatyana Tomashova (Russia) 3min 58.12sec
3, Maria Cioncan (Romania) 3min 58.39sec

A difficult beginning

Kelly Holmes was born on April 19 1970 in Pembury, in Kent. She did not have the easiest of starts in life. Kelly's parents were Pam Norman and her Jamaican boyfriend, Derrick Holmes. Pam was just 17 when she gave birth to Kelly.

Kelly stands with, from left to right, her father Derrick Holmes, her mother Pam and her stepfather Michel Norris, after receiving her MBE at Buckingham Palace in 1998.

Pam's own parents were unhappy at the arrival of their new, mixed-race grandchild and wanted Kelly to be adopted. In those days, many people of their generation disapproved of mixed-race relationships. Without her parents' support, Pam left home to stay with Derrick in London but the couple split up before Kelly's first birthday.

Now homeless, Pam had no choice but to put Kelly into a **children's home** and move back in with her parents. Pam visited as often as she could but Kelly remained in the home for 18 months. Pam eventually found a flat in south London and tried looking after Kelly herself, but holding down a job at the same time proved impossible. Kelly went back to the children's home when she was four.

Life finally began to settle down for Kelly when Pam met a new partner, Mick Morris. The three of them began living together in London as a family before moving to a house in Hildenborough, in Kent. In 1977, Pam and Mick were married. The same year, Kelly gained a half-brother when Kevin was born. In 1980, another brother, Stuart, arrived. Kelly loved her new family members and has remained close to them ever since.

Things were now starting to fall into place for Kelly. Even Pam's parents, Kelly's grandparents, had slowly come to accept her.

Kelly arrives at the premiere of the film 'Wimbledon' flanked by her brothers Kevin and Stuart.

WOW!

Kelly's mother visited her in the children's home as often as she could. When she tucked her into bed at night, Kelly would cry so much that her mother found it difficult to leave.

INSPIRATION

Kelly has always thought of Mick Morris as her 'dad' and they remain very close. In her **autobiography**, 'Black, White and Gold', Kelly describes Mick as "my support and my biggest fan".

Early promise

Kelly's first experience of sport was winning the egg-and-spoon and sack races at primary school. It was not until she went to secondary school that she realised she had a real talent for running. When she was 12 she entered her first inter-school **cross-country** race. She finished second, despite running in flimsy plimsolls.

TOP TIP

"You have to be very, very focused before a big race, especially in middle-distance running because it's so tactical. You may have the talent to win a race, but if you haven't thought it through properly, you won't win." Kelly Holmes

At the suggestion of her PE teacher, Kelly joined Tonbridge Athletics Club. The **coach** at the club was a man called Dave Arnold, who put her through a tough training programme. Kelly loved the hard work and was always keen to try something more demanding.

Kelly shows off her Olympic gold medals to her PE teacher, Debbie Page, during a visit to her old school, Hugh Christie Technical College in Tonbridge, Kent.

The following year, at the age of 13, Kelly won the 1500 metres race at the Kent Schools Championships and was chosen to represent Kent at the 1983 English Schools Championships in Plymouth. She won again, beating the previous year's champion. When she got home, Pam and Mick had decorated the house with flags.

Kelly continued to train hard with Dave Arnold and began to dream about being a world-class runner. Watching the 1984 Los Angeles Olympics on TV, she was inspired by the sight of British athlete Sebastian Coe winning the 1500 metres gold medal.

Kelly competed in her last English Schools Championships in 1987 and won the senior 1500 metres title. She was also picked to run in the 800 metres at the mini-Youth Olympics in Pappendal, Holland. To her amazement, she won. She was presented with a gold medal to the sound of 'God Save The Queen' and the noise of Pam and Mick shouting in the background.

INSPIRATION

'Watching the 1984 Games inspired me. Maybe one day I could become an Olympic champion too." – Kelly Holmes

Sebastian Coe wins gold in the 1500 metres at the 1984 Olympics in Los Angeles, USA, ahead of his GB team-mate Steve Cram, who took the silver medal. Coe's win was a big inspiration for Kelly.

Joining the Army

Ever since she was 14, Kelly had thought about joining the Army. A careers officer had visited her school and shown a video about Army life. From that moment, her ambition had been fired. She would combine her love of sport by becoming Army physical training instructor, or 'PTI'.

A couple of months before her 18th birthday Kelly took her final **oath** to join the Army. Despite her successes on the running track, she had decided to call a halt to her athletics career. Now she had a new life as Private Holmes.

INSPIRATION

"The whole **ethos** of the forces – the discipline and learning to fend for yourself – is the same as in athletics. You have to be confident and committed to your training."
Kelly Holmes

Kelly believes her time in the Army helped her to become a better athlete by teaching her the importance of discipline and hard work.

But life was not quite so ordered back home in Kent. Before joining the Army, Kelly had been distressed to learn that Pam and Mick had split up and that Pam was seeing another man called Gary. Later, she was even more upset when she found out Pam had married Gary without telling her. To complicate things further, Kelly had also discovered that her father, Derrick, had married and that she now had a half-sister, Lisa, and a half-brother, Danny.

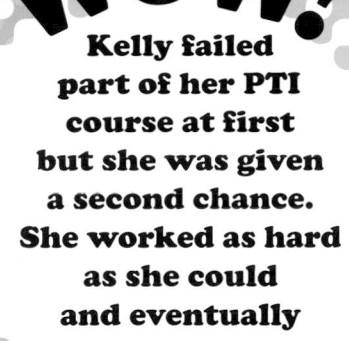

WOW!

Kelly failed part of her PTI course at first but she was given a second chance. She worked as hard as she could and eventually she passed.

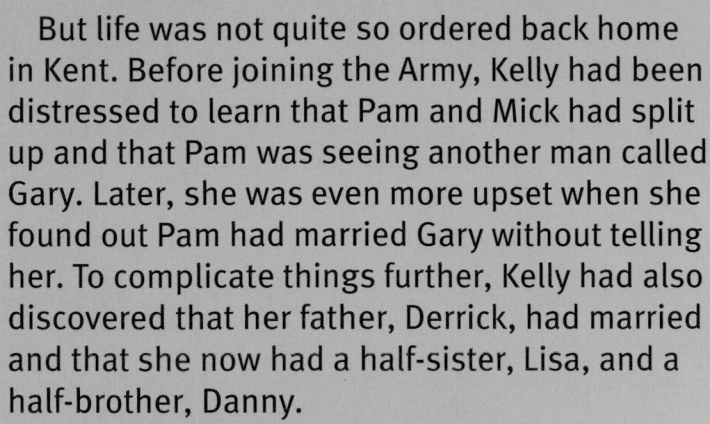

In the Army, Kelly began her new military life by learning to be a truck driver before she was given the chance to **qualify** as a PTI. The training was very difficult but by 1991 she had achieved her aim. Kelly was posted to the York **Garrison** as a PTI.

At her **passing-out day**, where she received her PTI qualification, Kelly had some visitors — her mother, Gary, and their new baby, Penny.

After starting as a truck driver in the Women's Royal Army Corps, Kelly rose through the ranks of the Army to become a Sergeant Class 1 PTI.

Back on track

In 1992, while still working at the York Garrison, Kelly sat down to watch the Barcelona Olympics on TV. One of the British athletes in action was Lisa York, who had been a rival of Kelly's at junior level. Kelly had a life-changing thought. If Lisa could make it to the Olympics, why couldn't she?

Since joining the Army, Kelly had been competing in some **inter-services** races and had started training at weekends outside the Garrison with an athletics coach, Wes Duncan. She decided that she would start to train more seriously.

She began running regularly for the Middlesex Ladies club and ended up winning the Southern Championships as well as the Inter-Services Championships. Although her Army career still came first, her athletics ambitions had returned.

WOW!

As well as a runner, Kelly was a blue belt in judo and even won the Army Judo Championship.

Kelly receives a tough workout as she runs through tyres during a training session in 1993.

In 1993, she entered the senior UK Championships at Crystal Palace. She won in a time of 2 minutes, 0.86 seconds that qualified her for the World Championships in Stuttgart, Germany, later that summer.

After another victory in her first ever **grand prix** in Stockholm, Sweden, Kelly was off to Germany. Although she failed to qualify for the 800 metres final, she set an English record of 1 minute 58.64 seconds in her semi-final.

Kelly was now an international athlete but she wanted more. She wanted to win medals. After teaming up again with her old coach, Dave Arnold, her wish came true in 1994. At the European Championships in Helsinki, Finland, she won her first senior medal — a silver in the 1500 metres. Weeks later, she competed in the 1500 metres at the Commonwealth Games in Victoria, Canada. This time she won gold.

TOP TIP

"Championships can be so overwhelming. There is nothing that can prepare you for them. The main thing to remember is that if you are good enough to get into the team, your only apprehension should be about how you are going to perform."
Kelly Holmes

After winning the women's 1500m final at the 1994 Commonwealth Games, Kelly is all smiles as she poses for the cameras with her gold medal.

injury strikes

Kelly's success on the track continued at the 1995 World Championships in Gothenburg, Sweden. She won a silver medal in the 1500 metres and a bronze in the 800 metres. A few weeks later, she broke the British 800 metres record in a race in Monaco with a time of 1 minute, 56.21 seconds.

Kelly was determined to train even harder as an athlete but she was also due to go on an exhausting, six-month PTI course. She was still committed to the Army but she decided to give up on her PTI ambitions. She was transferred to the Army Youth Team based in north London to help train teenagers. The new job gave her more time to for her own training.

Kelly shows her determination as she starts the 800m final at the 1995 World Championships at Gothenburg in Sweden. She went on to win the bronze medal.

WOW!

During an Army white-water canoeing exercise, Kelly capsized her canoe and was swept down the rapids before being thrown out of the water. She thought she was going to drown.

The highlight of 1996 was the Olympic Games in the American city of Atlanta. Unfortunately, Kelly's preparations for her first ever Olympics were affected by illness and injury.

Kelly had been suffering from stomach pains for several years. She had an operation at the end of 1995 but the pain continued. To make matters worse, two weeks before the start of the Olympics a bruise came up on her left shin and it felt painful to jog. A scan revealed that she had a **stress fracture.**

Doctors advised her not to run in Atlanta but Kelly refused to give up on her Olympic dream. After receiving pain-killing injections, she ran in both the 800 and 1500 metres, finishing fourth and 11th. Afterwards, her injured leg was put straight in a plaster cast.

Grimacing in pain, Kelly is beaten into fourth place in the 800m final at the Atlanta Olympics in 1996. The winner was Russian athlete Svetlana Masterkova (right).

TOP TIP

"You have to work very, very hard in middle-distance running because you have to have so many skills — strength, speed, **endurance**, power, tactical awareness and self belief."
Kelly Holmes

Despair turns to joy

Kelly's experience in Atlanta proved a turning point. It made her realise that she needed to dedicate herself to athletics if she was ever to win an Olympic gold medal. After 10 years of **military** service, she decided to leave the Army.

Kelly broke the British and Commonwealth 1500 metres records in Sheffield in June 1997 but her hopes of winning a gold medal at the World Championships in Athens were shattered by another injury. In the middle of the 1500 metres final, she tore the Achilles tendon in her left ankle. She hobbled away from the track in tears.

TOP TIP

"When you compete in a sport seriously you have to be careful with your diet and use food to help and to give you energy. Drinking water is important but having a balanced diet gives you everything you need to be healthy and strong."
Kelly Holmes

Pain and disappointment show on Kelly's face as she leaves the track after her 1500m race in Athens in 2007.

The injury proved serious and a whole year went by before Kelly was able to race again. She returned for the Commonwealth Games in Kuala Lumpur, Malaysia, and was delighted to win a silver medal in the 1500 metres. There was more good news at the end of 1998 when she received an **MBE** for her services to the British Army.

Kelly's injury problems persisted throughout 1999 and the start of 2000 — the year of the Sydney Olympics in Australia. Three months before the Games, she tore her right calf muscle in training. Kelly's spirits were very low. Was she ever going to fulfil her Olympic ambitions?

Thankfully, she still had time to recover. Although she was not fully fit, Kelly qualified for the 800 metres final in Sydney and then amazed herself by winning the bronze medal. After all her problems, she was overjoyed at the result. She was an Olympic medallist at last.

Kelly cannot contain her delight at winning her first Olympic medal — a bronze in the 800m in Sydney in 2000.

INSPIRATION

"If I got injured and I couldn't run, I'd still train. I'd go to the pool or the gym. I'd do everything else possible to keep myself fit."
Kelly Holmes

Highs and lows

After the high of Sydney, Kelly was brought down back to earth when she diagnosed with glandular fever and **chronic fatigue syndrome**. Despite her problems, Kelly was well enough to compete in the summer of 2001 and even ended up being ranked third in the world in the 800 metres.

Kelly's life at this time was a roller-coaster ride of ups and downs. At the end of the year she had to have an operation on her stomach. By the summer of 2002 she was on a high again, winning the 1500 metres gold medal at the Commonwealth Games in front of a **home crowd** in Manchester. It was one of the happiest victories of her career.

WOW!

Kelly's luggage went missing when she flew in for an 800 metres race in Gateshead in 2001. She had to borrow a pair of running spikes from another athlete but still managed to win the race.

A delighted Kelly celebrates after winning gold in the 1500m at the Commonwealth Games in 2002.

Fed up with so many injuries, Kelly then took a life-changing decision to travel to South Africa to train alongside Maria Mutola, an athlete from Mozambique who had won the 800 metres gold medal at the Sydney Olympics. Maria's American coach, Margo Jennings, agreed to coach Kelly as well.

The new training went very well and Kelly won a 1500 metres silver medal at the World Indoor Championships in Birmingham. But, on her return to South Africa, she was injured yet again. This time Kelly became so depressed that she locked herself in her bathroom and started to cut herself with a pair of scissors.

Thankfully, Kelly's injury and her mental state began to improve and she stopped cutting herself. After reaching rock bottom, she was soon experiencing another high. At the World Championships in Paris, Kelly finished second behind Maria in the 800 metres final. Her running career was back on track.

Kelly waves to the cheering crowd as she celebrates with 800m race-winner Maria Mutola at the 1993 World Championships in Paris, France.

Olympic glory

It was 2004. Olympic year. The Athens Games were fast approaching and, at long last, Kelly was free of injury. Even the constant stomach pains had stopped. Kelly was beginning to feel optimistic about her chances at the Olympics.

Before the Games, Kelly joined the rest of the British squad at a preparation camp in Cyprus. Her training went perfectly and she had never felt fitter. Although she had been planning to compete in only the 1500 metres in Athens, she decided to enter the 800 metres as well.

After winning her **heat** and semi-final, Kelly went to the start-line for the final of the Olympic 800 metres final on August 23rd 2004. Less than two minutes later, Kelly's lifelong dream had been fulfilled. With an incredible burst of speed in the final 200 metres, Kelly out-sprinted her rivals to win in a time of 1 minute, 56.38 seconds.

WOW!

After Kelly's 800 metres victory, she was helped out of her running spikes by Sebastian Coe, the athlete who inspired her Olympic dream when she was 14 years old.

With a lare surge of speed, Kelly powers past her opponents, including Maria Mutola (right) to win the 800m gold medal at the 2004 Olympics in Athens.

At first, Kelly could not believe she had won but when she looked up at the giant screen and saw the replay, she realised what she had done. Finally, she was an Olympic champion.

On August 28, Kelly made it a double celebration. Kelly was the favourite to win the 1500 metres final and this time she was in no doubt she had won. Racing away from her opponents, she crossed the finish line first in a British record of 3 minutes, 57.90 seconds. Now, with her two Olympic gold medals she had made history.

In honour of her double triumph, Kelly was chosen to carry the Union Jack at the Closing Ceremony. It was the perfect end to a perfect Olympic Games.

Sebastian Coe, Kelly's girlhood hero, presents her with the 800m gold medal at the Athens Olympics.

INSPIRATION

"You have to know what you want out of your sport. Ultimately, you have to have the thought inside you, 'I want to be the best'." Kelly Holmes

A nation celebrates

Kelly was unprepared for the scale of the reaction when she flew home to England. Her mother and the rest of her family met her at Gatwick Airport. Kelly was whisked off in a giant limousine and driven home to Kent where a surprise party awaited.

Two days later, Tonbridge Council organised an open-topped bus parade. About 15,000 people had been expected to turn up but, in the end, a crowd of 80,000 cheering fans packed the town, waving Union Jack flags.

Kelly was now a big celebrity and was invited to appear on TV programmes, including the Michael Parkinson Show, the EastEnders Christmas Special, At Home with the Kumars and the Ant and Dec Show. At the end of the year, Kelly was voted the BBC Sports Personality of the Year. It was the first of many awards.

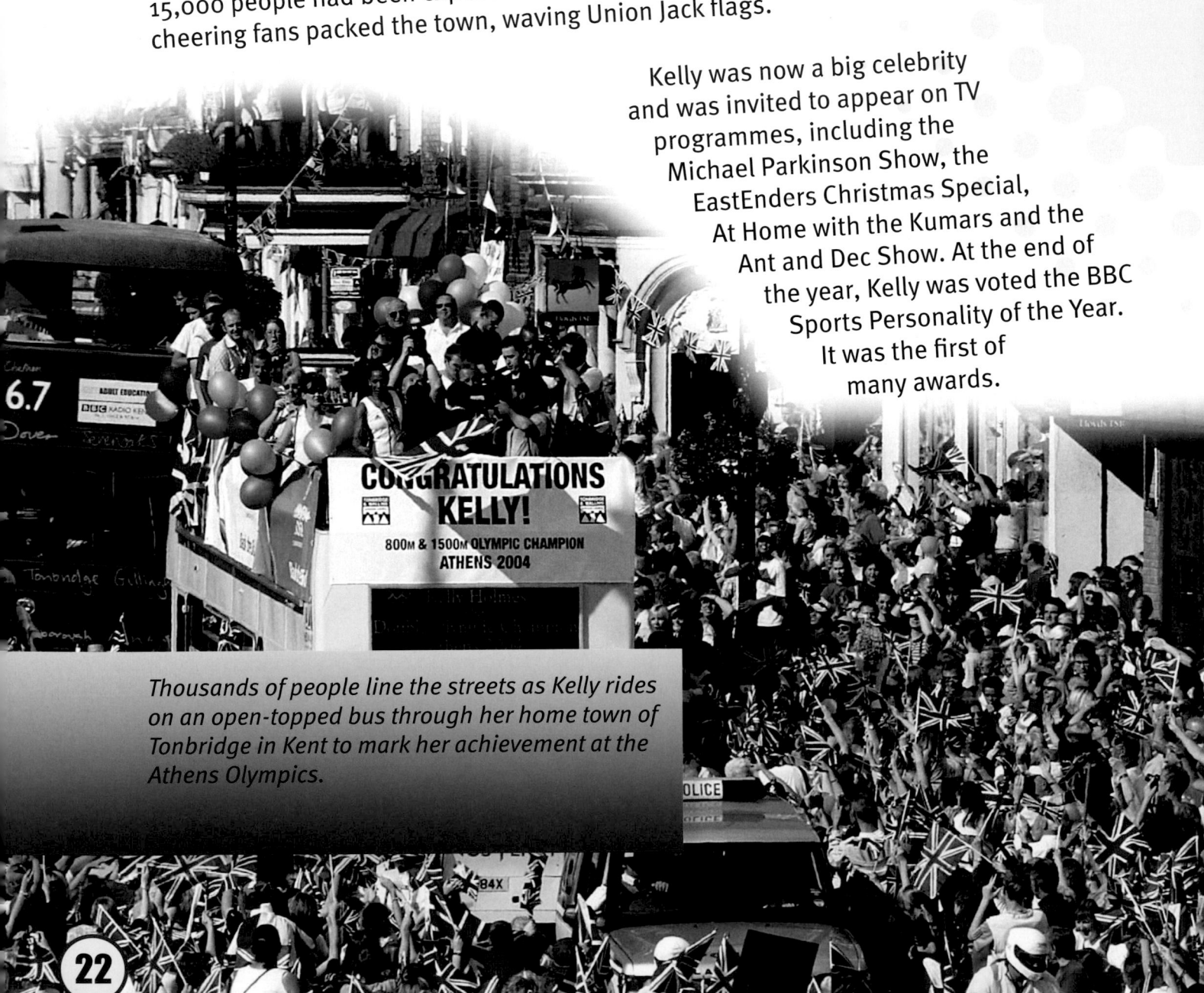

Thousands of people line the streets as Kelly rides on an open-topped bus through her home town of Tonbridge in Kent to mark her achievement at the Athens Olympics.

CONGRATULATIONS KELLY!
800M & 1500M OLYMPIC CHAMPION ATHENS 2004

The most important award came on March 9 2005 when Kelly visited Buckingham Palace. She had an appointment with the Queen, who presented Kelly with a Damehood in recognition of her sporting achievements.

Four months later, Kelly was back in central London celebrating with a large crowd in Trafalgar Square after London was announced as the host city for the 2012 Olympic Games. But, at the age of 35, Kelly's own sporting career was about to end. In August, she competed for the last time in a 800 metres race in Sheffield before retiring from running. Waving to the crowd, she bade an emotional farewell to her athletics career.

A proud moment for Kelly as she receives her Damehood in 2005.

INSPIRATION

"The Olympics has the ability to inspire people from so many walks of life, and so many abilities and disabilities, to get involved in sport." Kelly Holmes

HONOURS BOARD
Kelly's medal record

1994
Silver: 1500m, European Championships (Helsinki)
Gold: 1500m, Commonwealth Games (Victoria)

1995
Silver: 1500m, World Championships (Gothenburg)
Bronze: 800m, World Championships (Gothenburg)

1998
Silver: 1500m, Commonwealth Games (Kuala Lumpur)

2000
Bronze: 800m, Olympic Games (Sydney)
2002
Gold: 1500m, Commonwealth Games (Manchester)

Bronze: 800m, European Championships (Munich)

2003
Silver: 1500m, World Indoor Championships (Birmingham)
Silver: 800m, World Championships (Paris)

2004
Gold: 800m, Olympic Games (Athens)
Gold: 1500m, Olympic Games (Athens)

Life after running

A few months before the Athens Olympics, Kelly began her 'On Camp With Kelly' scheme. Since retiring from athletics, this has become an important part of her life. By passing on her own experiences, she is able to guide the careers of young, promising athletes and help them fulfil their potential.

INSPIRATION

"Kelly has helped me believe in myself. She gave me reassurance that I could be a good athlete," – Hannah England, 'On Camp With Kelly' member

Since 'On Camp' started, more than 60 British athletes have attended educational and training camps organised by Kelly in various parts of the world. Some of the young camp members have gone on to become international athletes themselves. Kelly plans to help even more up-and-coming runners in the future.

A group of young athletes, including Hannah England (far left) are put through their paces by Kelly at one of her 'On Camp' sessions.

Kelly has also set up the Dame Kelly Holmes (DKH) Legacy Trust, a charity that inspires young people to fulfil their talent in sport or in life by providing them with role models from top-level sport. Many of these are athletes at the end of their own careers, giving them a new role when they retire from competitive sport.

Since 2006, Kelly has been a National School Sport Champion, which involves visiting schools and attending events for teachers and young people. Her role is to inspire children of all abilities to play more sport and to encourage schools to provide at least four hours of sport and PE a week.

In 2009, Kelly was appointed president of Commonwealth Games England. The Commonwealth Games have been close to her heart ever since she won her first gold medal in Canada in 1994.

WOW!

An episode of Doctor Who is set in 'Dame Kelly Holmes Close' during the London 2012 Olympics.

As a National School Sport Champion, Kelly visits lots of schools to encourage children to do more physical exercise.

NATIONAL SCHOOL SPORT WEEK

NORWICH UNION
an AVIVA company

Youth Sport Trust

A day in the life of Kelly Holmes

Kelly's day always begins with a good breakfast. It is her most important meal of the day because she is often so busy she does not get another proper chance to eat. She has cereal, fruit, orange juice and sometimes toast.

If there is time, she will go for a run. Although she is no longer an athlete, keeping fit and staying healthy and energetic is still very important to Kelly. Then, on a typical day, it's off to visit a school in her role as National School Sport Champion.

The school has organised a Sports Festival and Kelly is met by a welcome party of young leaders before she is given a tour of the festival. After joining in with some activities, Kelly makes a short speech to the children.

WOW!

Kelly helped to come up with the idea for an annual "School Olympics", which the Government announced in June 2010.

Kelly gives advice to young athletes during an 'On Camp' training session in 2009 in Portugal.

Next stop is Kelly's office in London, where she has the chance to catch up with some emails and phone calls. One of her 'On Camp With Kelly' athletes needs some advice about her training programme, so Kelly gives her a ring to talk things through.

Then Kelly has a meeting about the Commonwealth Games. As president of Commonwealth Games England she is given an update on how her fund-raising campaign is going.

There is just enough time to change into her evening dress for an awards dinner in a central London hotel where she is due to make a speech and hand out prizes. It is gone midnight by the time she finally gets home.

WOW!

Kelly organised a cookery lesson for her 'On Camp with Kelly' athletes with TV chef Ainsley Harriott. Eating the correct food is very important if you want to be fit and healthy.

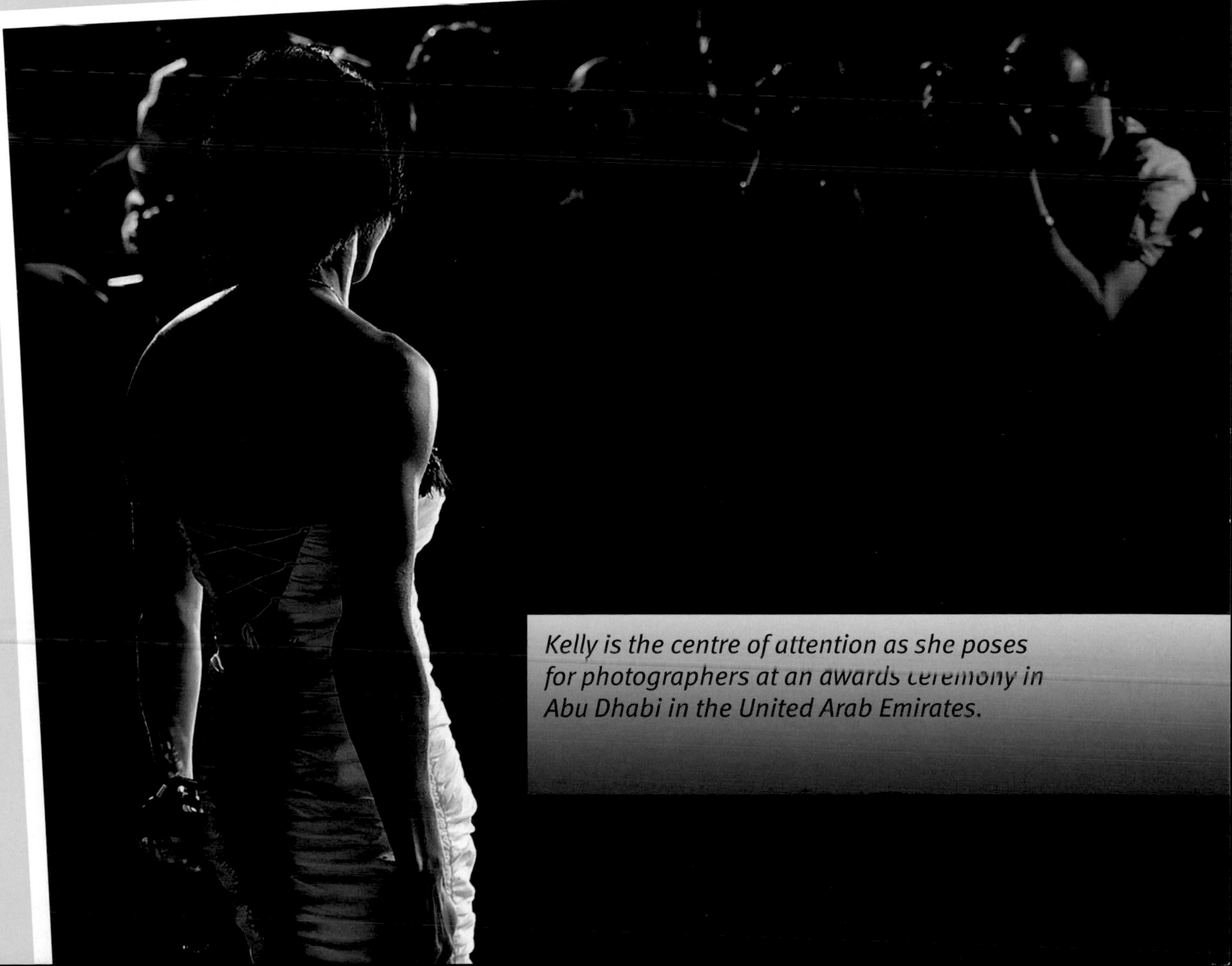

Kelly is the centre of attention as she poses for photographers at an awards ceremony in Abu Dhabi in the United Arab Emirates.

The impact of Kelly Holmes

From her difficult beginnings in a children's home, Kelly Holmes became a sporting heroine and Dame Commander of the British Empire. Her life shows what can be achieved through talent, hard work and, above all, determination. Throughout her career she suffered many setbacks but she never gave up on her dream.

Kelly signs autographs for eager fans on a visit to an England netball match as part of her role as president of Commonwealth Games England.

INSPIRATION

"A lot of people have tried it, few people have done it. In historic terms and athletic terms, what Kelly did was supreme." Sebastian Coe

Kelly's single-mindedness was obvious from her early days when she first joined her local athletics club and asked for harder training exercises. Even at the age of 12, she was determined to improve.

She showed the same sense of purpose when she joined the Army. Becoming a PTI was far from easy but Kelly knuckled down to her training and eventually achieved her goal.

But it was in Kelly's career as an athlete that she showed the spirit of a true champion. Although her talent was never in question, she was plagued constantly by injuries and illnesses. A less determined athlete would have been tempted to give up.

Kelly was not a quitter, though. Even when she was injured, she would find an alternative training exercise to keep herself fit. She never lost of sight of her goal of becoming an Olympic champion. Finally, at the age of 34, her dedication was rewarded when she arrived at the 2004 Athens Olympics in perfect physical shape. The rest is Olympic history.

Kelly is now passing on her own experiences to the next generation of athletes to help them fulfil their own potential. If they show anything like Kelly's determination to succeed, they should go a long way.

INSPIRATION

"I could have given up. I had depression, everything. But I felt in my heart one day it might happen. This is my life, what I've dreamt of forever. No one can ever take it away. I will always be Olympic champion." Kelly Holmes

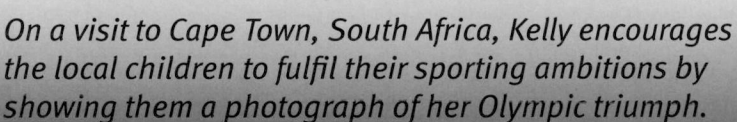

On a visit to Cape Town, South Africa, Kelly encourages the local children to fulfil their sporting ambitions by showing them a photograph of her Olympic triumph.

Have you got what it takes to be an Olympic champion?

1) Can you cope with hard, physical work, even when it gets painful?
a) Yes, I'm prepared to put up with pain to achieve my goals.
b) It depends how painful. I can just about handle a stitch.
c) No way. If it's painful, I'm not interested.

2) Do you have the self-discipline to turn up to regular training sessions?
a) Yes. If I make a commitment, I stick to it.
b) Maybe, but sometimes I get enthusiastic about something and then lose interest later.
c) I prefer to do my own thing. I don't like my life to be too organised.

3) Are you prepared to stick to a healthy diet, even if that means giving up your favourite foods?
a) Yes. I know that eating properly will improve my performance.
b) I could try, but I would find it very difficult to give up certain foods.
c) No, I only eat food that I really like.

4) Would you be happy to give up your leisure time to train and rest properly?
a) Yes. I would rather be doing something in my free time anyway.
b) I would be prepared to give up some of my free time, but not all of it.
c) My leisure time is very precious to me. I would find it hard to give that up.

5) Are you able to follow the instructions of your coach, even if you disagree with them?
a) Yes. The coach is more experienced than me and knows best.
b) I'm prepared to try, but it depends on the instructions.
c) No, I'm not very good at taking orders.

6) When you are playing sport, how important is it for you to win?
a) Very. I really hate losing. I always try to do everything I can to win.
b) I like to win, but it's not the be-all and end-all. You can't win all the time.
c) I'm not that bothered about winning. Some people take sport far too seriously.

7) What would you do if you got injured and were unable to train properly?
a) Ask my coach for training exercises that I could do without making the injury worse.
b) I'd wait until the injury healed before doing any more exercise.
c) I'd do all the things you're not allowed to do when you are training.

RESULTS

Mostly As: You have the right kind of attitude to become an Olympic champion. Choose the sport that best suits your talent.

Mostly Bs: You are clearly interested in sport but you need to find something you really enjoy. Perhaps you'll get more serious about it later.

Mostly Cs: You might not be that sporty, but physical exercise is good for your health and lots of fun. Why not give it a try!

Glossary

autobiography A book about a person's life, written by that person.

children's home A place where children are looked after if their parents have died or are unable to care for them themselves.

chronic fatigue syndrome A condition that causes the sufferer to feel extremely tired for a long period.

coach A trainer or fitness adviser.

cross-country A running race held on open countryside.

endurance Staying power or the ability to keep going when the body feels tired.

ethos Set of values or beliefs.

form Physical condition or fitness.

garrison A place where soldiers are stationed.

grand prix An important athletics event. Literally in French a 'big prize' competition.

heat A qualifying race in which the top finishers go through to the next round.

home crowd Spectators from the place where the event is taking place.

immune system The system in the body that fights off infection.

inter-services Describing an event that takes place between the different armed services such as the Army, Navy or Air Force.

MBE Member of the British Empire medal. This is a special award given by the Queen to reward someone for their service.

military Related to the army or the armed services.

oath A solemn promise.

passing-out day The day when military recruits complete their training course.

qualify Make it through to the next round of a competition.

rapids Part of a river that is very rough and fast-flowing.

running spikes Athletes' shoes with metal spikes on the soles to grip the track.

straight The uncurved part of an athletics track.

stress fracture A thin crack in a bone caused by wear and tear.

white-water canoeing Riding in a canoe on a fast-flowing river where the water froths and bubbles.

Index

INSPIRATIONAL LIVES

Contents of new titles in the series

Kelly Holmes
978 0 7502 6480 8

Golden girl
A difficult beginning
Early promise
Joining the Army
Back on track
Injury strikes
Despair turns to joy
Highs and lows
Olympic glory
A nation celebrates
Life after running
A day in the life of Kelly Holmes
The impact of Kelly Holmes
Have you got what it takes to be
  an Olympic champion?

Lewis Hamilton
978 0 7502 6481 5

World Champion!
Growing up
Starting karting
Moving home
Making sacrifices
Joining McLaren
Success and setbacks
Life in GP2
Welcome to F1
Racing rivalries
A day in the life of Lewis Hamilton
The ups and downs of being
  a celebrity
The impact of Lewis Hamilton
Have you got what it takes to be
  a motor racing champion?

Tony Hawk
978 0 7502 6483 9

"The best day of my life"
A hyperactive child
Bitten by the boarding bug
Getting good
Turning pro
High school star
Building Birdhouse
Ups and downs
Video game star
Business booms
Giving something back
A day in the life of Tony Hawk
The impact of Tony Hawk
Have you got what it takes to be
  a pro skateboarder?

Usain Bolt
978 0 7502 6482 2

The world's fastest human
A lively child
Success comes early
Reality check
Time to rebuild
The world takes notice
Olympic superstar
Return of a hero
Lightning strikes twice
Awards and injuries
A day in the life of Usain Bolt
An inspiration to others
The impact of Usain Bolt
Have you got what it takes to be
  a record-breaking athlete?

WAYLAND